Self Visions
of Poetry in Parables

Self Visions

of

Poetry

in

Parables

Return too a New Beginning

Andre Pullen

A Vision Publishing/*Chicago*

Copyright © 2002 by Andre Pullen
A Vision Publishing Chicago Heights, Illinois

All Rights Reserved.
No part of this book may be reproduced in any form
Or held in an information storage and retrieval systems
Without permission in writing from A Vision Publishing
Except by a reviewer,
Who may quote brief passages in a review

ISBN 0-9718281-0-5

Printed in the United States of America

Direct any inquiries to
A Vision Publishing
P.O. Box 900
Chicago Heights, Il 60412

Dedication

This book is dedicated to Self, for the remembrance of times past and the establishment of times yet to come. I also dedicate this book to every soul that has, that is and that will face the test of time and tribulation. I pray that this book will provide a continuous renewal to my spirit and also everyone who reads it.

Acknowledgement

      For the writing of this book I would like to acknowledge God the Father, my refuge in the times of tribulation, God the Son, my deliverer from my sinful self and God the Holy Spirit, my guide to understanding. I would like too further acknowledge His word, which is the beginning of all creation including myself and this book. Without Thy word I would not have had the faith to trust in that which I do not understand, nor would I've known my ways were sinful, neither would I've known where to find refuge when faced with the tests of temptation that I could not handle alone. In all my ways I thank You oh God and pray forever that Your word lives in me and also in my brothers.

Self Vision (I AM)

Andre Pullen (1 with 3)

Lamentations 3

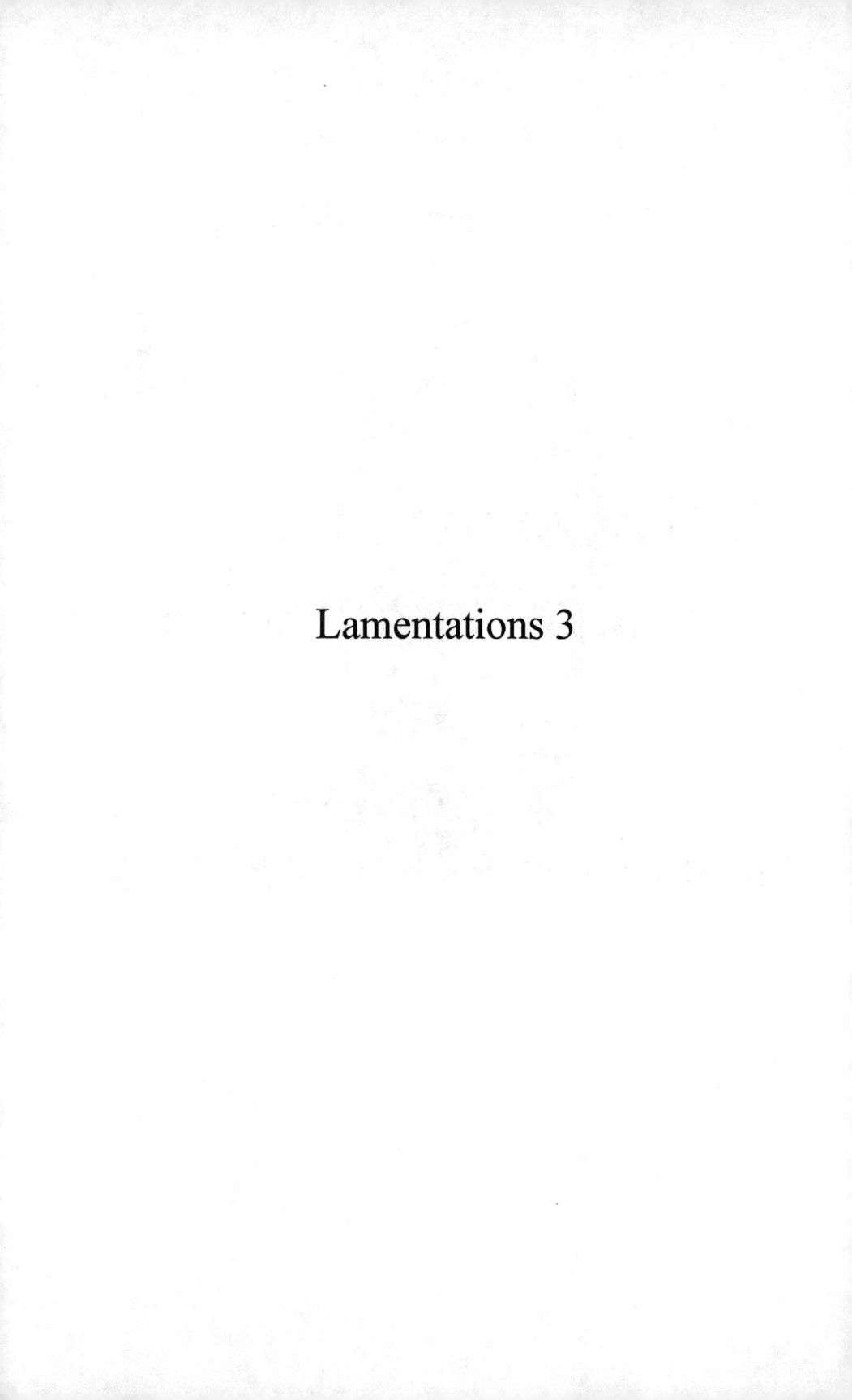

Self Visions of
Poetry in Parables

Return Too A New Beginning

Contents

3. Preface
5. Intro
6. Life Testament
7. Prophecy of Self—Seeking Wisdom
8. Committed tto Self—Finding Life
9. Self Understanding—Finding Jesus
10. Selfs Poem—Seeking Self
11. Childless Father—Seeking Peace
12. Forgive Me Jr. For My Sins—Finding Forgiveness
13. the Light—Seeking the Son
14. Let Faith Make Sense—Seeking the Light
15. Lost—Seeking the Way
16. Selfs Prison—Seeking the Cross
17. Freedom—Finding the Law
18. Forgive Me For My Sins—Seeking Clarity
19. Belongings—Seeking Meaning
20. Answers—Seeking Knowledge
21. Thinking—Seeking the Spirit
22. Summer Time—Seeking Sacrifice
23. The Telling of Selfs Time—Finding Christ
24. Myself—Seeking Direction
25. Facing Myself—I AM Finding I AM
26. Jr.—Finding Clarity
27. Time Will Tell—Seeking I AM
28. Todays Tears—Seeking Joy
29. Selfs Bed—Seeking Unity
30. Tears—Seeking Life
31. Faces—I AM Seeking I AM
32. Time—Seeking Commitment
33. These Tears Belong Too This Day—Finding Life
34. Self Sometimes Writes—Finding the Word
35. I AM Unstoppable—Seeking Salvation
36. The Best Wrote This—Finding the Light
37. Unstoppable—Finding Salvation
38. Commitment—Finding Time
39. Unafraid—Seeking Power
40. Who is Conceited—Finding Strength
41. Unstoppable Best—Finding Self
42. I AM Sent Me—Seeking God
43. Words—Seeking the Word

44. A Letter too Self
45. Return Too A New Beginning
46. Love Testament
47. Parables—Seeking One
48. Can I Love You
49. Finding One
50. 100% Commitment—Seeking Strength
51. Paradise—Finding Paradise
52. Amazing Woman—Finding Wisdom
53. Revolution of Self—Seeking Change
54. Addicted too Love—Finding Foundation
55. For Your Love—Seeking Love
56. I Need You—Seeking the Shepherd
57. Evolution of Self—Finding Change
58. I Shall Sing For You—Seeking the Song
59. If This World Were Mine—Seeking Foundation
60. Can You Tell Me What I'm Suppose To Do—Seeking Assistance
61. Beloved—Finding Vision
62. Psalms—Finding One
63. I Give You My Heart—Finding Knowledge
64. Lies—Seeking the Truth
65. My Lost Love—Finding the Spirit
66. Sucker For Love—Seeking Vision
67. Revelations of Self—Seeking Completion
68. Too Be 100% Committed—Finding Assistance
69. Lifes Biggest Decision—Finding I AM
70. Sucker For My Lost Love—I AM Finding Vision
71. Please Spare Me No Pain—Finding the Way
72. Questions
73. Seeking Answers
74. Genesis of Self—Finding Completion
75. Return Too A New Beginning
76. Testimony Too Self

Preface

This book is dedicated to Self as a documentation of a proclamation of who I am. I hope to explain too myself the vision of who I am is not who I found myself to be when I look into the mirror, for the mirror only cast the reflection of what I want to see. When actually what I see is controlled by my mind. Now of course there would be a need for something to control the mind, for a mind out of control will loose itself as I have come to know through experience. In order that I may find that which controls me, my soul, is the blessed spirit that dwells inside my body. My body is only the representation of time I use to show myself in a form that my mind can understand and evolve to levels of the soul, but the mind cannot reach the highest level of the soul that is god while it is stuck in the dimensions of the body. I pray this book will indeed reveal who I am too myself, so that I may know God in this life time and exist with Him in the time that is yet to come.

Introduction

Andre Pullen, the man known too be **Self Vision.**
I would like first to thank you for taking the time to acknowledge my book "Self Visions of Poetry in Parables." I sincerely hope this book will be a blessing too you as it has been a blessing for me to write it. When I first started writing, I was 12 years old and in the seventh grade. "The Bigg Butt" was my first piece to be recorded. Since then my love for writing has grown tremendously. During my years at the University of Illinois Champaign/Urbana, I began to study my craft and perfect my skills. As the time passed by I watched my talent mature slowly as I grew older. I began not only writing about women and relationships, but also other aspects of life and its experiences. I soon noticed how gifted a writer I was and that I had to share my gifts with the world. If I truly wanted to thank God for my blessings.

This book is a representation of my own experiences, thoughts and feelings in relation to life. My desire for you to read it is not so that you can know me. I wish that you acknowledge your own self through me, by adding your personal thoughts and feelings to the word pictures that I have painted describing life.

Enjoy
Self Vision

Self Visions of Poetry in Parables

LIFE TESTAMENT

Return Too A New Beginning

Prophecy of Self

I live for you
If you live for me
If your love be true
My love be true too you
I'd eat, sleep and breathe for you
If you'd eat, sleep and breathe for me
If the love be true
Our love be true
Dreaming about change
Imagine that me and you

Seeking Wisdom

Thank You oh God for all Your grace and glory
Lord I pray for change so that I may make a difference
In this world, bless me Lord to not be self-centered
But God-centered so that I may attain self-knowledge
And the essence of salvation most important knowledge
Of You my glorious God, thank You Lord for Your light
For without it I am lost, but with it I do see the way
Dear God, I pray that You reveal the work that
Has been appointed for Thy faithful servant
So that I may forever follow Thee

Committed too Self

Locked in a commitment to life
A journey into the unknown
Living to know the meaning of it all
It's going to take strength to remain strong
Throughout the struggle of man to survive
But I shall live for one reason
Self, for after death
There is only the remembrance of who I AM
Which in time will be forgotten until
I AM remembered again by the heart of man
I will rejoice then in living for Self
For I AM all that there is and
After I AM gone I will be all that remains
On a journey of a life time into the unknown
Committed to live forever locked up
In all that there is an existence of life

Finding Life

Thank You oh God for giving me purpose
Bless me with the wisdom too understand Thy ways
For on the road to understanding what is right
I have stumbled a countless number of times over what is wrong
Lord do not let me compromise what I know of Self
For in debate I create disunity between self and Christ
My Lord and Savior, I pray to You oh God that
Now will be my time to act out Your will and purpose
Bless my surroundings so they will not hinder me from
Becoming useful to You my Lord, grant me the discipline
To remain obedient in all things
So that I do not become caught up in what is wrong
On the road to what is right and all along the way
I will be singing praises in Thy holy name

Self Understanding

I'm trying to catch up
With understanding but
I keep landing at a dead end
Still I search an unending search
One day I know I'll see
Self Vision inside of me
Thanks too Love and Understanding
I AM complete

Finding Jesus

Thank You Lord for all Your blessings
It is You oh God who bleeds my heart and knows
My love for Thee is not imaginable, I pray to You
My Lord for strength to obey Your will so that
I may discern truth, thank You Lord for knowledge
And understanding to love wisdom all in Self
I pray that I will be able to pass on all that I have
To my brother so that he too can know and understand
The love of God and I will not be left with the anxiety
Of being empty for another part of me has been made full
Allowing me still to give full praise to a glorious God

Selfs Poem

Dis is Selfs poem bout Self and dats me Self
Dees words don't have to made cents too you
As long as day make cents to Self and dats me Self
Cause my connotations might not be da same
As da denotation in Websters but dats OK
Cause I'm not Webster I'm Self and
Dis is Selfs poem bout Self and dats me Self
But don't judge me judge yourself because
You don't know me you only no dees words
And I doubt that yo name is Webster
So how can you say who or what I AM
Try figuring out who you are and you'll
See you don't make as much cents as you think
But why am I talking bout you when dis poem is bout
Me Self

Seeking Self

Thank You Lord for blessing me to be Self
I pray to You oh God that others too will see
And know Self for those whom think
They know me best knows me least of all
You my Lord art the only one who truly knows Self
Lord I pray for knowledge, wisdom and understanding
So that I who thinks shall not know least
But will come to know best of all, bless me
Lord with patience for I know my time is coming
But I know not of the day and bless the day Lord
For the day as everyday I give back to You my Lord

Childless Father

I am a childless father, for I have no child
each day my son cries inside of me, for he can not cry aloud
and although I don't have the stress of diapers to change
or another mouth to feed, I now have the burden of your soul
inside of me, so as you cry I cry and as I bleed you bleed
for it was I who chose to take your life when
you were only a seed, but life is a game of choices and I wish
I could teach you to choose wisely and timely, for no one
can play forever, but a winner is clever enough to make his worst
hand his best hand, for it is the man that plays the cards he's dealt
and I'm so sorry I felt that you wasn't my winner, but myself
I was born a sinner in this crazy world that made me
not want to be bothered so now I reap the pain
of a childless father. Only if I knew the things that I know now
then maybe life would be different, but I am only a man
and I can not change the past. I can only pray to my Lord
that my first may become my last, and if I could I would
bring you into this evil place. Until then rest in peace
my unplayed Ace.

Seeking Peace

Thank You Lord for this day I pray to You oh God
To take away my anxiety and distress so that
I may not live in misery but with great delight
And joyfully praise Your holy name, I pray to You
My Lord to bring peace to my starving heart so that
I may feed Your understanding to a multiple of people
And they too will hold Your name in all its glory
For You are the only true God, all praises
I will forever sing to my supplier of salvation

Forgive Me Jr. For My Sins

Dear Lord, can you save me
From these elicit dreams, dreams so wild
So confused, I know I'm going crazy
So please can you save me
From these thoughts in my head of an unborn child
Can you forgive me for my sins
These dreams these dreams how long will they last
I wasn't always like this but the world has made me
Haunted by mistakes made so long in the past
A creature so insane he could kill his own baby
These dreams these dreams I wish they go away
So Lord, I pray you to save me
A second chance is what I beg
But I'll be stuck with these dreams 'til my dying day
So Lord please can you save me

Finding Forgiveness

Thank You oh God for being forever forgiving
For it is inevitable that I fall short of Your standards
Lord I pray to set me free from these choking chains
That are fighting to steal my breath, thank You dear God
For humbling my heart so that I may forgive those who sin
Against me, I pray that You enlighten the path I walk
So that I may follow Thy example to be like Christ
And when my time for persecution comes I can pray
Father forgive them

The Light

It travels like a secret at night
The frightening scare that tares through my brain
The pain of being insane as the game goes on
I try my best to be strong
To hold on to the sand that leads me into the land of glory
And as the story flows on
It flips into a song sung straight through my soul
Trying to show me the light
That shines so bright I shade my eyes
For fear I may loose my sight
On this ruff road but riders ride
'til we reach the heavenly skies
Say it takes a thousand tries
Some it takes a thousand lives
'til finally they see the truth
And the day Self-LUV dies
Let the records show
That there were living proof

Seeking the Son

Thank You oh God for your timeless law, Lord I pray
That You remove all distractions from me so that
I may refocus my life on Christ Jesus the Lord
Of my light and salvation, bless me oh God to be one
With Christ too concern myself with only one thing
And I will not be found asleep when it is time
For me to make my mark in history, Lord I pray
For patience so that I shall not be so anxious
As to not understand what is on the heart of my God
Bless me to hear and bear witness to the truth
Of Jesus Christ the Son of the Heavenly Father

Let Faith Make Sense

I cry out as a lost soul searching for the answer
Trying my best to avoid sin for it destroys me like Cancer
I search for the narrow road that leads me into the light
Relying only on my faith for I am blind even with sight
As I walk the twisted paths not a moment shall I fear
Being blessed with all my senses I need not my ears to hear
I worry not that I may stumble for it is inevitable
The pain I feel the grace of God makes me stronger
As the light of the Lord is revealed

Seeking the Light

Thank You oh God for allowing me to serve Thee
Lord I pray that You do not allow my faith to fall
For it is Your altar in which my world stands on
And without You it is impossible to be right so
I AM left drifting aimlessly as if in space lost
Searching for a space to settle but the only place
I find peace and pure pleasure is in the heart of You
My Lord, I pray You stay with me oh God
For You are the support that saves me
From being swallowed by the sea of sinners

Lost

Twisted and confused afraid to loose, but what
For I have nothing or maybe afraid to loose
What I don't have I can hear someone laugh
In the distant winds as my paths are entangled
By sins that twist my ways into a never ending maze
And never releasing the madness that's in my mind
And never freeing me from the chains that enslave
My brain like cocaine oh I must be a crack head
Probably more since in that head than in mine
It's so hard to do the time when I'm blinded by faith
I just can't wait, so eager to see with my own eyes

Seeking the Way

Thank You Lord for this day, bless me oh God
With understanding to see and strength too change
My sinful ways that dwindles my dreams to nothingness
And entangles my life into a twisted ball of confusion
A trapped illusion that dwindles my dreams to nothingness
Lord I pray that You release me from these relentless
Chains of sin that struggles to link me into its interwoven
Ways of wickedness and rob me of Your heavenly glory
Be with me Lord and guide my steps
In the way of the righteous

Selfs Prison

Dear Lord, they've got me trapped in Selfs Prison
Trying to diminish Self Vision but today I confirm
Selfs mission through a conversation with God
He knows I'm wishing to be saved from the sea
That I'm fishing, thank You Lord for listening
To my prayers, which has made me stronger but
I'm afraid I can no longer wait my fate I can't escape
Please do it now if you must choose to hate
Tomorrow may be to late for I'm about to unleash
The gate to Selfs Prison

Seeking the Cross

Thank You oh God for another chance to serve You
The One and only true God, bless me Lord to choose wisely
As I walk in the way of Thy will I pray for strength
So that I shall not surrender my soul to the sufferings
That are required to bring others into Christian maturity
Thank You oh God for sending us Jesus the Christ
I pray to You my Lord to show me my cross so that
I may follow Christ the Lord of my light
Supplier of my salvation and
King of Thy holy kingdom

Freedom

To have freewill
To think and dream freely
To fly without being high is to be free
I hope to be free one day
Nothing holding you back
From having a dream too
How hard does it seem
To you too be free
I hope you become free one day
What would you do if you were free
Do you know what it's like to be free
When will you see
You don't need eyes to be free
I'll share with you some it's in me
The desire to be free
From all restraints and restrictions
No afflictions or addictions
To hinder my will to be free
I shall will myself free one day

Finding the Law

Thank You Lord for love and understanding
Bless me oh God with the knowledge of Your law
So that I may live my life by Your standards
Thank You Lord for saving me from my sins
That lead me to satans sanctuary
Please protect my paths dear God so that I will be free
To experience the fullest pleasure of life
And not be robbed of the delight and joys
That You have insured for me,
Forever I will live following Thy timeless law
With Self knowledge

Forgive Me For My Sins

Dear Lord, can you save me
So confused, I know I'm going crazy
So please can you save me
Can you forgive me for my sins
Cause I wasn't always like this
But the world has made me
Into a creature so insane
He could kill his own baby
But that's a choice I will never understand
The decision made as an innocent child
Still affects me as a man
So Lord will you save me
From these treacherous days and torturous nights
That rips out my soul and destroys my life
So Lord I pray you to save me
A second chance is what I beg
So please can you save me

Seeking Clarity

Thank You Lord for helping me to see the light of spring
In the darkest of winters, I pray to You oh God
For Your continuous support for the hand of evil
Does to reach out too me in attempts to destroy Your kingdom
Bless me with the strength my Lord to work diligently
Through all seasons so that there will be no time
For dormancy and each day will be as a day in autumn
For it is true I have no closure except within You
My Lord, for Your purpose I pray that today will be
My time and season to spring into action according to
Your will and never fall back into the dormant trap of winter
Thank You Lord for hearing my cries

Belongings

My heart, belongs to You my Lord
My soul, belongs too You my Lord
My spirit, belongs too You my Lord
My mind, belongs too You my Lord
My flesh, belongs too You my Lord
My life, belongs too You my Lord
I have nothing and want nothing
But, to live for You my Lord

Seeking Meaning

Thank You oh God for all Your grace and glory
Lord I pray for change so that I may make sense
Of the bills you have bestowed upon me
What shall I do my Lord? I pray to You oh God
To reveal the work that You have predestined
For Thy faithful servant, for I live only to work for Thee
So Your kingdom shall stand in all its glory forever
All praises I sing for Thee Lord of my mind, body and soul
The gate keeper of my spirit and my reason for living

Answers

Lord, where can I find peace in this evil world
Who can you trust in this evil world
What should I do in this evil world
How will I find peace in this evil world
Lord, when will I know

Seeking Knowledge

Thank You Lord for blessing me with roots that
Have remained firmly planted in Thy word
I pray for Your continuous support oh God
So that I may not fall prey to the ungodly
The ones who despise against me
For I am truly Your servant and it has become
Evident that I can not stand unless I stand on your ground
My Lord, bless my paths make them straight
And enlightened with righteousness
So that I may spread the truth of Thy name
All praises I sing to Thee forever and ever

Thinking

Sometimes I close my eyes so I can think
Put some ice in a glass and pour out a drink
And reminisce and reminisce about the old days
My old ways, the twisted ways I used to have
Sometimes it makes me sad sometimes it makes me laugh
As I look back over the path I used to walk
How I used to act and talk in the past
How things changed and they so fast
Left only with memories but how long will they last
Definitely not forever but possibly for a blink
Something to make you think should I open
My eyes or should I finish the drink

Seeking the Spirit

Thank You Lord for this day, bless me oh God
To be wise in my ways with confidence where
I will not have the need to anticipate what outcome
Will occur but be tolerant to accept the consequences
For my actions, I pray to You Lord for wisdom
That I may understand Your ways to prevent me
From being lost in the past so that I may advance
In the future and spread the word of Thee almighty God
Across the land

Summer Time

Summer is slowly approaching
My dreams I can clearly see
But its so hard to keep on hoping
My heart is worn out from wishing
To attain the love that I'm missing
I pray I will be able to find
Without my vision is blind and
My mind is left wide open
Making it hard to keep on hoping
But summer is slowly approaching and
In the light I will surely see
My dreams as clear as can be

Seeking Sacrifice

Thank You oh heavenly Father for choosing me
To serve Thee, I pray that You strengthen my flesh
For I have become weakened by the ways in which
I travel, do not let me be taken by temptation nor
Fooled by false prophets, but let the light that
You have given me shine on the path of my brother
Who walks in darkness deceiving his self of the truth
That we are all one in the body of Christ, bless me
Dear God to live by example granting all my gifts
To those who do not see so that they too will witness
The greatness of our God and give praise on to Thee
For all Your glory and I too shall rejoice in Thy name
For I live only to serve Thee heavenly Father

The Telling of Selfs Time

It's my birthday a celebration of my first day
Dear Lord, forgive my soul a young man in the face
I made it another year and I got to go on despite my fear
My time is so old I almost wish I could digress
I shed a tear cause Lord knows I'm not happy here
But it's still so much time that have not been yet
So each night I cry but I must continue so I try
To maintain long enough for things to change
There are still so many people that haven't realized
There own sins yet, I feel this my year so wish me well
Lord where does it begin where does it end at
Can't predict the future but time will tell
I guess it will depend on how you spend your time
So this time next year I hope I'm here
But if I'm not don't shed a tear
Lord knows I'm not happy here

Finding Christ

Thank You my wise and wonderful God for showing me
The way of sin and suffering, without which I would not
Be able to see the ways of the righteous man as separate
From the wicked without separating the two as men
I sing praises to You Lord for allowing me to work
In Thy holy name, also for the blessings You have
Bestowed upon me, I pray that I remain obedient to Your will
And not walk away from what is right nor judge my brother
For his wrongs 'les I loose my ability to lead others
Out of darkness so that they too may sing
Thank God for the days that we have suffered

Myself

My life is nothing but lonely days and empty nights
That pierce my soul like a bed of spikes
Each day my pain increases from all the drama I face
And still I have to come home to an empty place
My home is a trunk, extremely small in size
But it seems like a mansion in my eyes
For all I see is emptiness across from wall to wall
There is only a telephone which no one seems to call
The radio is playing, but my attention is focused
On my mirror because he is giving me advice
To make things clearer, D'marco tells me
Most of my hurdles are the ones I bring
And to get my life together and change a few things
So that once this happens it will be to my delight
There will be no more lonely days and empty nights

Seeking Direction

Thank You oh God for Thy word which gives life
To my spirit and meaning too my existence, bless me
Lord with definition so that I will not be misinterpreted
By myself or others, but be regarded with respect
To the exact degree that You have made me, I pray to Thee
My Lord too impose Thy will on my ways so that my way
Will be identical to the desires of You oh God
Allowing others to use me as a conductor
So their path will lead to the glory of God

Facing Myself

As I look into this mirror
My life is nothing but lonely days and empty nights
What is this I see oh it's a face
That pierces my soul like a bed of spikes
Is it really me I don't understand
Each day my pain increase from all the drama I face
I can't see myself am I afraid to be me
Still I have to come home to an empty place
Is it because I AM someone else
The radio is playing, but my attention is focused
On my mirror as I stare into these eyes
He gives me advice to make things clearer
I begin to understand a guy who never was a child
D'marco tells me most of my hurdles are the ones I bring
I AM now a grown man, but is this man really me
I need to get my life together and change a few things
Am I someone else as this face gets blurred
So that once this happens it will be to my delight
I see myself as I look into this mirror
There will be no more lonely days and empty nights

I AM Finding I AM

Thank You Lord for the troubling times that I face
Without them I would remain weak and
Never understanding my way to Christ
For unless I know the ways of the crooked paths
As well as the straight and narrow I could never
Distinguish the two nor could I lead any lost souls
Out of the darkness, bless me oh God
To keep focused on my mission and during the times
In which I stumble, correct my steps Lord
So I can learn the way from which I came

Jr.

Elicit dreams, dreams so wild
Thoughts in my head of an unborn child
These dreams these dreams, how long will they last
Haunted by mistakes made so long in the past
These dreams these dreams, unable to suppress
How I regret the choice I made that put me in this mess
These dreams these dreams, I wish they go away
But I'll be stuck with these dreams 'til my dying day

Finding Clarity

Thank You Lord for having mercy on my soul
I pray to You oh God to refresh my spirit for my soul
Has grown weary in the winds of change, Lord I pray
That You remain by my side for I can not recover
On my own it is the power of Your presence
Which rejuvenates my soul so that I become
As radiant as the sun, thank You Lord for each day
For without a day there is only darkness and who knows
What evil lurks in the depths of darkness, but I do know
It is the light of the Lord that illuminates the endeavors
Of evil doers so that Your sheep do not fall
Into a pit of destruction

Time Will Tell

It's my birthday, a celebration of my first day
I made it another year and I got to go on despite my fear
I shed a tear cause Lord knows I'm not happy here
So each night I cry, but I must continue so I try
To maintain long enough for things to change
I feel this my year so wish me well
Can't predict the future, but time will tell
So this time next year I hope I'm here
But if I'm not don't shed a tear
Cause Lord knows I'm not happy here

Seeking I AM

Thank You oh God for allowing me to praise
Your holy name and for the changes You have made
In my life, Lord I pray that You bless this day for me
That I may shine like the sun upon Your world and others
Will see me as I see myself then they will trust
In Your name, bless those who see me so that they
Become as I AM not in the ways of flesh, but in the way
Of Thee most holy for not all my ways are my ways
In taking on the ways of another would also lead to
Taking his suffering also, bless me oh God to rejoice
In my own suffering and give Thy praise back to Thee

Todays Tears

My eyes are filled with sorrow and
My heart is filled with pain
Hoping for change tomorrow
Today just seems the same
My tears wash away my grief
But do not remove the pain
Today my heart is filled with sorrow
For my burden still remains
I search for a place of peace
So my soul can finally rest
Praying to finish the game each day
Is still a test, it's so hard to see clearly
In the midst a stormy rain
Praying for change tomorrow
Hoping for no more pain

Seeking Joy

Thank You Lord for the sacrifice that You have made
For my sins, I pray for the same strength to make
Sacrifices in my life so that others will benefit through
My pain and strife so they may glorify Thy name
Bless me dear God to not become overwhelmed by
The obstacles in life that are intended to make me stronger
Let me understand these events so that I may learn
From these experiences that prepare me for the future
In each day to come bless me to sing praises
To Thee true God

Selfs Bed

In the darkness I lie restless on an empty bed
Starving for understanding and in fear of knowing
The truth for I'm to scared of becoming full
Will I ever be satisfied is what I mostly crave
Praying throughout the night too make it through the days
Where satan is always there tempting me in his evil ways
He knows my bed is empty and understanding is
What I crave through my fear he gains his entry
To defile what's in my head trying to keep me
In the darkness on this lonely bed
Will I find a place to rest, please Lord help me
To understand fill me with the truth for
My life is in your hands

Seeking Unity

Thank You Lord for listening and providing the answers
To my prayers, bless me with the wisdom to understand
The purpose that You have intended for Thy faithful
Servant, do not let me remain lost in the darkness as to
Be fooled into believing that my prayers have not been
Answered, bless me with the insight to rejoice as I wait
For understanding of that which I already know but
At the present time I do not comprehend the parts that
Make the whole one, grant me the remembrance of the parts
That I may reunite that which has been forgotten
With the light and all will be found leaving nothing
Lost in the darkness

Tears

As my tears flow rapid like rivers I can't stop the shivers
As the hawk blows harsh winds against my skin
I feel as if I'll never win at this crazy game
Even if things seem the same, I know it's impossible
For them to have not changed, but in the end
I know what remains, the pain in my heart and the stress
In my brain

Seeking Life

Thank You Lord for being my Shepard, I pray
To You oh God as I pass through the valley of the shadow
Of death to not allow my surroundings to cause me
To suffer nor sin too seize my soul let Thy rod and staff
Save me dear God from the sinners that seek a true saint
To sacrifice to satan, Lord bless me to fear no evil
For fear makes it impossible to faithfully follow You
Lord Thank You for being there in the darkest of days
For without You oh God my life is lulled by temptation
Leading me to die a sinners death

Faces'

As I look into this mirror, what is this I see
Oh, it's a face but is it really me
I don't understand why I can't see myself
Is it because I'm afraid to be me or to be someone else
As I stare into these eyes I began to understand
It's a guy who never was a child but is now a grown man
But is this man really me or is it someone else
As this face gets blurred then I see myself

I AM Seeking I AM

Thank You oh God for blessing me, Lord I pray
For wisdom so that I will be able to observe
The extraordinary things that happen in the midst
Of the ordinary for everything is known and caused by
God to be extraordinary, bless me Lord to not fall
Into one of the common traps of man causing me to miss
The message and the opportunity to have an encounter
With God

Time

Dear Lord, forgive my soul, a young man
In the face but my time is so old I almost
Wish I could digress my progress it causes
So much stress about to explode my mental
Index, but its still so much time that have not
Been yet so many people that haven't realized
Their own sins yet Lord where does it begin at
Where does it end at I guess its going to
Depend on how you spend your time

Seeking Commitment

Thank You oh God for being with me, Lord I pray
For strength so that I will never again doubt
The almighty creator by doubting myself, bless me
Oh God to act as a mediator and pass on to the people
The understanding that You have so graciously bestowed
Upon me, Lord I pray that You have mercy on my soul
As I strive for the unattainable and miserably fail the test
Of temptation, but despite of my failures bless me
Oh God in knowing that You are forever with me
That I may rejoice in offering praise to a magnificent God

These Tears Belong too This Day

My eyes are filled with sorrow and my heart
Is filled with pain, as my tears flow rapid like rivers
I can't stop the shivers, so I pray for change tomorrow
Today just seems the same
As the hawk blows harsh winds against my skin
My tears wash away my grief, but do not remove the pain
I feel as if I'll never win at this crazy game
Today my heart is filled with sorrow for
My burden still remains even if things seem the same
I know it's impossible, so I search for a place of peace
So my soul can finally rest
For some things have to change, but in the end
I'm praying to finish the game each day is still a test
I do know what remains the pain in my heart
So its so hard to see clearly in the midst a stormy rain
With all the stress that's in my brain
So I pray for change tomorrow hoping for no more pain

Finding God

Thank You Lord for not forsaking Thy faithful servant
Bless me dear God to rejoice in the changes of the wind
And not weep over my ways that have been blown away
I pray for Your continuous support oh God for the devil
Has yet to cease trying to steal my soul for he knows that
You have called upon me to serve Thee each day my Lord
I am preyed upon by the devils predators trying to
Tempt me to test my God bless me with the words to rebuke
The devils spirits and retain the hope of Thy people so
That the world will realize the presence of
Thee Almighty God here on earth

Self Writes Sometimes

Sometimes I write to be free, maybe to find me lost
Or trapped in one thought I escape by moving on into
A song of sweet melodious rhythms that soothe my soul
Like an ice cold smoothie on a hot and humid day
And oh what pain does my soul have more than
These words can express, the more I release the more
Stress I gain disguised in soft notes is a hardened pain
A cancer to my brain and a thief to my soul
So to whom does my soul belong to God
Self or too this song maybe
I'll find the answer trapped in these words
Or lost in another thought trying to escape
What has been written and trying too be free
Sometime in Selfs lifetime

Finding the Word

Thank You oh God for the gifts
That were promised before my time
I pray for understanding of the things that
Have been written so that I may be sure of the way
In which I walk and not be fooled into following false Gods
To loose my treasure, fill my soul with the body of Christ
My Lord renewing my inner Self so that I may continue
Singing praises in Thy Holy name and Your people
Will witness the incomprehensible events with understanding
In the presence of Thee Holy One

I AM Unstoppable

You can not stop me, for I am unstoppable
You can not knock me down, for I will only get back up
You can not keep me trapped, for I refuse to be stuck
You can not stop me, for I am unstoppable
You can not hold me down, for I will not allow you
You can not limit me, for I choose not to be bound
You can not stop me, for I am unstoppable
You can not contain me, for I am too quick
You can not restrain me, for I am too strong
You can not stop me, for I am unstoppable
You can not control me, for I will never submit
You can not terminate me, for I work through the Lord
You can not stop me, for I am unstoppable
You can not corrupt me, for I have pure faith
You can not contaminate me, for I have a cleansed spirit
You can not stop me, for I am unstoppable
You can not change my destiny, for I direct my own fate
You can not change me, for I love who I am
You can not stop me, for I am unstoppable
You can not inhibit my dreams, for I desire to have them all
You can not fend me off, for I will only keep coming
You can not stop me, for I am unstoppable
You can not keep me quiet, for I know more ways to speak
You can not deny me, for I will not be forsaken
You can not stop me, for I am unstoppable
I am unstoppable and you can not stop me

Seeking Salvation

Thank You oh God for Your living word, bless me Lord
With knowledge of the scriptures so that I may gain
Knowledge of Thee and have comfort in knowing that
Every outcome happens according to Thy plan, I pray
That I will be able to control the events that confuse me
And forgive those whom abandon me and also help those
That criticize and misunderstand, Lord please do not
Let me fail for my life is devoted to Thee
And my obedience is to Your law

The Best Wrote This

I believe I'm the best but
I don't have to be better than you
Besides you ain't even in my category
When I look into this mirror
Ain't nobody finer than me
I'm fresh like new money
Everybody want to get their
Hands on me cause I'm the best
But you don't have to believe me
As long as you believe yourself
Cause the best wrote this

Finding the Light

Thank You oh God for Your light, Lord I pray that
I may shine as a testimony to Your great glory and
The darkness that does cause those around me to sleep
Will be displaced and they too will wake up
In the brilliance of You my Lord, thank You oh God
For the dawn of a new day for I AM a witness to Your son
Christ Jesus the light that has dispelled the darkness
From my life so that I may become a light to the world
And a disciple for Christ so that others will glorify
Thy Holy name of Thou who art in heaven

Unstoppable

I am unstoppable, that means I can't be stopped
Working through achievement until I reach the top
Cause I am unstoppable, that means I refuse to stop
Striving to be the best, cause perfect I'm not
But I am unstoppable, that means I won't be stopped
Working to control everything until I got the world on lock
Cause I am unstoppable, that means I can't be stopped

Finding Salvation

Thank You Lord for saving my soul from satan
And securing my faith in Thee, watch over me oh God
For satan is always scouting in attempts to seduce me
To join his squad of sinners, Lord I pray that You assist me
For on my own I can not defeat temptation, bless me
Oh heavenly Father to not be so selfish as to not assisting
My brothers who are in need to be saved for everything
I have has been given to me through Jesus Christ
My Lord and Savior

Commitment

Commitment in its essence is dedication
It takes dedication to achieve a goal
A want, a need or whatever your heart desires
It takes giving, even if you have to give
Everything you have, or for what reasons
Would you have for being committed
You have to trust that you will not fail
And believe in the reason you are committed

Finding Time

Thank You Lord for Self Vision, bless me dear God
To withstand the suffering that awaits along my path
I pray for the strength to change all moments
In which I suffer into times where I rejoice and accept
Even my pain as a gift from God, as of this day Lord
I shall no longer accept satan into my life as neither
Cause nor effect for my circumstances even though
All my choices may not be right I pray they lead me
To Your will which has been perfectly planned since
The creation of time and 'til my time on earth ends
My life I shall devote to praising Thee

Unafraid

I put you beneath the ground fear
I spit on you fear
I stand on top of your ugly head fear
Fear you are what I despise
I repel you with all my strength
I will no longer run from you fear
You are my slave now
If I ever see your head again
So help me God
I'm going to choke the life out of you
For I AM unafraid

Seeking Power

Thank You Lord for blessing me
Without You I have no power but
An abundance of fear, let me not be
Afraid my Lord, but empower me with
The strength to receive and obey
Thy will that leads me the right way out of
The twisted ways of the wicked
Infinite praises I sing for You my Lord
For without You I have no song to sing
All praises I sing for You oh God
The Father of my soul and spirit
The Emancipator of fear and
The Appointer of power

Who Is Conceited

I am a confident person, I have full confidence in myself
Because I have a confident attitude
I am so confident in my appearance
That nearly all compliments
Are still insults to my unmatching sex appeal
I am confident in my abilities to accomplish everything
I am confident that I am capable of making
My worst hand my best hand, I am confident that
I am a genius, I am confident that
I am gifted, I am confident that
I am blessed because I have full confidence in my faith
I am confident that there is no man greater than I
I am confident that I come from a blood line of
Kings among Kings
I am confident that you reap what you sow
I am confident that I will never loose
As long as I am willing to give it all
I am confident that the Lord speaks too me
I am confident that the Lord has extended
His hand too me time and time again
I am confident that my flesh will die
But my heart and soul will live forever
I am confident that one day you will see me
Just as I see myself
I even speak with confidence
Judge me not for by your judgments
You too shall be judged

Finding Strength

Thank You Lord for blessing me to have so much flavor
I pray to You Lord to use me too season the souls
Of sinners so that they too shall see You oh God shinning
Down upon us and will then learn to savor the flavor
Of Thy Savior and let them not become salty against
Your servant who has been sent to save the world from sin
Unless they too learn they have become salty against You
Oh God I pray for all those who seek signs to see the truth
Which is so easily seen through faith in You my Lord

Unstoppable Best

I am unstoppable that means I can't be stopped
That's why I believe that I am the best
So I work through achievement until I reach the top
But I don't have to be better than you
Cause I'm unstoppable that means I refuse to stop
Besides you ain't even in my category
I am the best but of course perfect I'm not
When I look into this mirror ain't nobody finer than me
I'm unstoppable that means I won't be stopped
I'm like new money fresh everybody want
To get their hands on me cause I'm the best
That's why I work to control everything
Until I got the world on lock
But you don't have to believe me
As long as you believe yourself
Cause I'm unstoppable that means I can't be stopped
And the best wrote this too

Finding Self

Thank You oh God for choosing me
Bless me Lord to be everything You have required
Dear God I pray for determination so that I shall not stumble
In my steps nor cease striving to attain perfection
Thank You Lord for the truth I now see
That it is for Your purpose that I suffer with Christ
And though I suffer in my heart I still rejoice
For You are with me always and forever
I shall sing praises to Thee anywhere, at any time
And under any conditions

I AM Sent Me

I am a writer not by choice by voice
I am a poet not by trying by crying
I am a slave not by self by wealth
I am a king not by earth by birth
I am God not by being by seeing
I am a witness not by fuss by trust
I am a saint not by giving by forgiving
I am a sinner not by living by dying
I am an animal not by feature by creature
I am huge not by size by prize
I am old not by age by stage
I am black not by face by race
I am a winner not by success by best
I am unstoppable not by going by showing
I am an addict not by addiction by affliction
I am a messenger not by message by passage
I am a poet not by trying by crying
I am a writer not by choice by voice
I am who I am
For I am has sent me
To be who I am

Seeking God

Thank You oh God for forever being with me
Thy faithful servant I AM although I AM not
When I AM alone nothing but emptiness a man
That does not exist without God I AM lost in an illusion
Of what is not searching for what is reality the truth of
God I pray too set me free from the illusion so that
I may find God in the existence of man to be
Full of nothing for I AM everything when I AM all one
Although I AM Thy faithful servant I thank You oh God
For forever being with me so that I may sing praises
Onto Thee for You are truly worthy to be praised

Words

What does a word mean
Do they mean like they sound
All grumpy or something more cheerful
What does a word mean
Do they mean what they say all the time
What about love then, who has the answer for that
What does a word mean
Does it depend on how it's spelled
On one level you'd be the same backwards
Would that mean you're not going no where
How would you get ahead then
What do words mean when you put them together
If you were levelheaded
Would you be able to go places then
What level would you go to for head then
Would you be going up or down
If you're going to the top
Will you take me with you
I want too find out what these words mean

Seeking the Word

Thank You my Lord for Your word
Bless me Oh God with knowledge and
Understanding of the scriptures so that
I will not be bewildered by life circumstances
That arise to bring me down, be my stronghold
My Lord, for in troubling times I take refuge
In Your word, for in my heart I know that
Your word is the truth that burns within me
I pray to You my Lord, too bless me with
Wisdom to spread the fire that burns deep
Within my heart and soul, thank You Lord
For opening my eyes so that I may discern truth

A Letter too Self

I too have a dream of unity and peace. I too fight for freedom from the oppressive forces of this world. My dreams are never ending, but always fulfilling every moment of the day. Today I declare my dream too be like Christ, the essence of perfection. As I prepare this document my mind is focused on the future of who I Am. This letter is the tangible evidence that I offer myself to the world as I am. Many people doubt my words and abilities because they lack understanding, but for no longer shall I hold myself back because of disbelief from others. Dear God, activate in me the ability to understand time and the patience too control it so that I may live out my dreams of being free.

Return
Too
A
New
Beginning

Self Visions
of
Poetry in Parables

LOVE
TESTAMENT

Return Too A New Beginning

Parables

Life is a dream that I live for you
I will live for you if you live for me
I'd give the whole world if your love be true
If your love be true then my love be true to you
What would I do? I'd eat, sleep and breathe for you
I'd eat, sleep and breathe for you
If you'd eat, sleep and breathe for me
I'd change your whole world if the love be true
If the love be true then our love be true
Imagine that me and you dreaming about change
Dreaming about change can you imagine that me and you

Seeking One

Thank You oh God for not allowing my needs
To go unsatisfied, bless me to be content with my gifts
And not desire in excess, for the things that I want
But do not have I want only for selfish reasons
I pray that Thee glorious God
Make Thy way the center of my life so that
I may have balance and not be easily blown off coarse
By the winds of change, thank You Lord for the changes
You have blessed me to understand, I pray for
The strength too testify to Thy greatness
So I may be a living testimony for the power of Christ

Can I Love You

I can give you nights of passion and days of pleasure
Show you the pot of gold in the worst of weather
But, can I love you
I can give you days of pleasure and nights of passion
The world can be yours just by asking
But, can I love you
I can pay your telephone bill, pay your visa bill
As long as you want me I will even stay and chill
But, can I love you
I can give you that big house on the hill
With what ever fence you like
But, can I love you
I can give you a knew walk-in closet wardrobe
Enough bling to make a blind man want shade
But, can I love you
I can give you 10 million dollars
If you want it another ten and another one
But, can I love you
I can calm your nerves and massage your brain
Change your world; take away your pain
But, can I love you
I can massage your brain and calm your nerves
Give you everything you feel you deserve
But, can I love you
I can give you the truth to set you free
All the time you want to be with me
But, can I love you
I can give you your dreams; let you make the rules too
The game, if you can love me as you love yourself
Then I can love you just the same

Finding Love

Thank You Lord for teaching me how to love
I pray to You oh God to let Your love overflow through me
Into the lives of others so they too will see my Lord
In all Your glory praise Thy holy name
Thank You dear God for Your unending love
That has saved me from the snares of sinners
Thousands of times so I shall sing thousands of praises
In Thy holy name, all honor I give to You oh God
My heart, my head and keeper of my heaven

100% Commitment

One hundred percent commitment is what it takes
For us to stand in this aisle and join our fate
Oh, I'm nervous now but I can't wait
To lift up that veil and see your face
But it's not just your pretty face that I love
You can start from your feet and go through all the above
You're so much like a blessing that floated down
From the skies again I thank You Lord for hearing my cries
And sending me a woman to whom I'm so perfectly fitted
And blessing me with the strength to devote my love to her
And become one hundred percent committed

Seeking Strength

Thank You oh God for allowing me to serve Thee
I pray to You my gracious Lord to be forever forgiving
Towards Thy faithful servant though I knowingly fall
Into temptation, I unknowingly tempt others into the same sins
Bless me oh God to stand tall and not assist others too fall
By following my actions, I thank You Lord for allowing
Me to see the pits that lie ahead in my path, please
Protect me dear God from the winds of change that blows
In the direction of the pit in attempts to push me
Past the edge, Lord bless me to keep my head
So that nothing may over take me

Paradise

Come travel with me to this magical land
To reach paradise is my plan
This journey may cause a little stress
And a little pain
But I will always be there to calm your nerves
And massage your brain
It may seem unreal
And you may think you are dreaming
As I show you things you wouldn't
Believe you are seeing
And take you to places you only dreamed of being
It's going to be hard to reach this magical land
But you only need to believe
Because I know we can
So come be my queen
And you'll soon see
All your dreams become reality

Finding the Way

Thank You Lord for humbling my heart so that my life
Would be filled with faith freeing me from wanting
Anything outside of You my Lord for I only wish
To graze in Your green pastures for all that You provide
Is pleasing to me, thank You Lord for being my shepherd
And leading me in the way of the righteous, Lord I pray
That You do not allow me to stray into sin
By the temptations of men for my flesh is weak
But my strength lies within my heart
Along with You my Lord

Amazing Woman

Woman, it's amazing what you do to me
Who would ever imagine girl you and me
Creeping off midnight rendezvous of pure ecstasy
You set my soul at ease just by standing next to me
I feel so blessed to be in these shoes with the chance
To spend eternity, I'm so confused Lord what's
My destiny I got this hunger inside as a man that
Craves this woman to rest next to me inside my bed
But can I truly trust these thoughts inside my head
And I'm constantly hearing something saying
You can't be scared to live what you get is what you give
You can't keep these feelings hid from yourself
You know even with money in your pockets
In your hearts the true wealth and finally
I opened up my eyes and I could plainly see
Woman, everything you do still amazes me

Finding Wisdom

Thank You Lord for the salvation You have blessed me
To see, I pray for perseverance dear God that I may
Be stead fast in Thy word so that I may be prepared to walk
The path of Christ, bless me oh God to not become
Bewildered by burning bushes that fail to be consumed
By the fire, but give me the confidence to observe Christ
By my side during each circumstance that seem
Confusing To my finite mind
Thank You Lord for my knowledge

Revolution of Self

Life is a dream
I'd give the whole world
What would I do
I'd change your whole world
Imagine that me and you
I live for you
If your love be true
I'd eat, sleep and breathe for you
If the love be true
Dreaming about change

Seeking Change

Thank You Lord for having mercy on my soul
I pray to You oh God too let Your will be lived
Through me as the truth for the love in my heart
Holds true to Your word, Lord I pray for answers
To the promises that You have made so that wisdom
Shall become clear in my sight and the way of Thy will
I shall follow, though I may stumble I pray
I don't fall through the days of sin for I live with men
Do not allow me to be discouraged or impatient Lord
For with all my faith I trust in You

Addicted to Love

I call this girl a drug, but in a good way
Since she made me fall in love in only one day
From the moment I seen her I knew I would be
Addicted to her love for all eternity
I have become depressed with my failure
For I have yet to obtain my prize, as my heart
Grieves with pain each time I look into her eyes
But I've come to accept my lost love although my pain
Worsens everyday, I am forced to regain my strength
Each night when I pray to my Lord and Savior that
One day I'll be able to bring great joy to this young girls
Life, one chance is all I ask one chance is all I need
For me to win her love and set my soul at ease

Finding Foundation

Thank You oh God for allowing me to discern the truth
Bless me Lord with faith to withstand any test
And surpass all temptation, I pray for endurance
To make it through the trials of life, I ask that You
Strengthen my mind and spirit though my flesh
Remains weak and in constant need of guidance
For with my own eyes I am led astray and with
My own ears I am deceived but, through my faith
I smell, taste and grasp hold of the victory
That has already been won, thank You Lord for giving me
Enough sense to have faith in not only the greatest
But the least of all things

For Your Love

I'd set out to unlock all the mysteries of the world
For the key to your heart
I'd cut myself in half for you to be my better part
I'd reach up and grab the sun if you needed light to see
And carry you across the world if you wanted to be with me
I'd work as a slave if I could just hold your hand
And confront the devil face to face too be your man
I'd wait a thousand lifetimes to witness one of your smiles
For one kiss from your lips I'd walk a million miles
I'd live in humility for the rest of my life
Infinite wars I'd battle to have you as my wife
I'd build you pyramids from the ground to the skies
For a glance of your beauty with my own eyes
I'd give all of my organs to sustain your health
And forfeit my winning lottery ticket worth infinite wealth
I'd cut out my tongue and gouge out my eyes
If I could heal your pain and hear your cries
I'd put myself through torture for you to have
A moment of peace and wait for you to receive me
Inside the belly of the beast
I'd do any and everything for your love
There is nothing I wouldn't do for your love

Seeking Love

Thank You Lord for supplying me with an abundance
Of love leading into life salvation, I pray to You oh God
For appreciation that I may live and love all blessings
That are bestowed on to me and not have the desire
For anything outside the body of Christ, bless me Lord
With Your grace so that I may give back
To Thy wonderful works in this world and
Give honor to Thy name causing each soul
To acknowledge the one and only true God

I Need You

It seems you're always in my dreams and I want you to
Fill my waking hours, when you're close to me
I can feel your magic powers, when ever I 'm not near you
A sense of emptiness starts to grow, but when I'm close
By you my world is filled with the glow when I come home
In the evening I'm still thinking of you if we would
Have never met I don't know what I would do I guess
That's why my thoughts keep telling me
How much I need you

Seeking the Shepherd

Thank You oh God for being forever forgiving
Lord I pray for endurance and strength to bare
My own load in times of discomfort, bless me oh God
To find Thee for You are the only comfort that I need
I pray You guide my steps oh God
Without You I am weak and easily trampled over
But with You I am strong and my strides are long and fast
Allowing me to hastily race for Your kingdom
And sing praises of glory for Thy victory

Evolution of Self

I live for you
If your love be true
I'd eat, sleep and breathe for you
If the love be true
Dreaming about change
If you live for me
My love be true to you
If you'd eat, sleep and breathe for me
Our love be true
Imagine that me and you

Finding Change

Thank You oh God for sending Your son Christ Jesus
Lord I pray for the authority to minister to the people
Of the world and for the power too perform miracles
In the light of the Lord, bless me dear God
With obedience to remain focused on my mission
To supply salvation too all those that are sent to me
Lord I pray that I will not be allowed to be distracted
Or preoccupied with self so that I be of no use
In ministering to those whom You have sent to me
On this day let me reconfirm that You shall be forever
With me Thy faithful servant

I Shall Sing For You

How I wish I could sing
'Til days end I would sing for you
Melodious rhythms I would bring for you
In psalms of praise I would thank you
For the sunshine rays you bring too me
On cloudy days I wish I could sing
I would sing forever for you

Seeking the Song

Thank You Lord for this day, bless me oh God
With a renewed heart and restored devotion to Thy word
So that I may continue being sensitive and also attentive
To Thy will and purpose, I pray to Thee merciful God
To separate Thy faithful servant from the evil and ungodly
Influences of this world that work to harden out my heart
Against my glorious God and also to my brothers
Bless me dear God with all Your power giving me
The strength to stand up to the misguided souls
Of this world that walk with wickedness and deceit
In their hearts and grant me the mercy too forgive
Those who wage war with Self so that I can share
With them the wisdom that has been given to us all

If This World Were Mine

If this world were mine
I'd wish I could share it with you
All my joyous times
I'd wish I could cherish with you
If this world were mine
I'd give it all just to see you smile
All my meaningless treasures
I'd live without to see you smile
If this world were mine
I'd make you my queen
All your worries and troubles
I'd take away for my queen
If this world were mine
I'd share it with you
Yeah, if this world were mine
It would be yours too

Seeking Foundation

Thank You oh God for not forsaking Thy faithful servant
Bless me Lord to share the love that has been shown to me
Please do not allow me to become preoccupied
With my own needs oh masterful God I pray that You
Provide an angel to oversee my ways and correct
My worries that cause me to stumble be my strength Lord
For You are all the support that I need
To keep from falling into a death caused by sin
I diligently pray to Thee oh God to lift me up
So that I can shine like the sun

Can You Tell Me What I'm Suppose To Do

Hey miss lady, can you tell me what I'm suppose to do
When you got a man I understand, but I still want too
Get close to you I'm not trying to break up a happy home
So I pop champagne and pour out a toast for you
And your man the lucky man who has the chance
To make you his wife so I wish you well, the finest things
The best in life and in my prayers, I pray for you
That he treats you right and his love is true
But, I'm on the outside looking in
So can you please tell me what am I suppose to do?

Seeking Assistance

Thank You oh God for the Holy Spirit, Lord I pray
For strength for my flesh is weak and is always in need
Of restoration, bless me dear God with Your presence
So as my flesh falls to temptation my spirit shall not
Surrender, but remain solidified as one in the body of Christ
Thank You Lord for lending ear to my prayers, I pray You
Make me alert and watchful as I pray so that I will not
Be found asleep during the time that holds
The most meaning in my life

Beloved

As my heart craves your eyes like
The stars that light up my world
In the midst of darkness I wait for the sun to rise
Bringing illumination to those eyes so that the truth
Will be seen in the way of the righteous
The wicked will then fall in their own web of deceit
Only to escape by faith for freedom follows
The denial of oneself to be led out of the darkness
And to my Beloved my world I give to you
Too have what your heart craves anything under
The stars so that my eye will not be covered
By darkness and your world will not be left without light

Finding Vision

Thank You Lord for opening my eyes, bless me oh God
To be alert spiritually making me aware of
The dangers around my family and self
Lord I pray for attention to Your word so that
My soul may be lifted up and I can shed encouragement
Too lift the souls of others, thank You dear God
For hearing my prayers, bless me with diligence
In acting on Your command and may I
Not falter once in my mission

Psalms

Life is a dream I live for you
I'd give the whole world if your love be true
What would I do? I'd eat, sleep and breathe for you
I'd change your whole world if the love be true
Imagine that me and you dreaming about change
I live for you if you live for me
If your love be true my love be true to you
I'd eat, sleep and breathe for you
If you'd eat, sleep and breathe for me
If the love be true our love be true
Dreaming about change imagine that me and you

Finding One

Thank You Lord for Your love, it is from Your love
That I know how too love others, but my mind
Can not comprehend how to love unconditionally
For the desires of my flesh interferes with the emotions
Of my soul causing war inside my mind
I pray too understand the vision of love that is
Inside of me so that I may become a living example to others
And they will see Self in a new light too be one
With everything and separate from nothing
For I AM all that there is and in me there is
Nothing but love, thank You Lord
For allowing me to understand Selfs Vision

I Give You My Heart

I give you my   Heaven
                    Earth
            All
                Ring
                        Teachings

Finding Knowledge

Thank You Lord for the wisdom that has been
So generously blessed upon me, I pray for guidance oh God
As I follow Christ my Lord and Savior let my eyes
Be opened so that I may lead Thy people to the way
Of love and understanding and we will all witness the truth
Of Thy vision, bless me Lord to be wise in making decisions
That affect not only me but also those around me
Let those in need come to me my Lord and together
We will travel on to Thee

Lies

I wanted to stop lying
Because I was looking for love
That's funny I was lost
In a loop of love once
It cost me a whole lot
All because of lies we drifted apart
If I knew how it would have ended
I would have changed it from the start
Will I make that same mistake again
And break two peoples hearts
I'd be lying if I said I wouldn't
And I'm trying to stop lying

Seeking the Truth

Thank You Lord for the truth, I pray to You oh God
That I may experience the truth in my life
So that I may recognize the power of God
Bless me Lord with discipline that I may be
Obedient in Thy word and not surrender to evil spirits
That attempt to trap me in their lies, bless me
To spread the truth of Your word oh God to those
That practice lies so that they may witness a revelation
And get prepared for a revolution

My Lost Love

My love and I were like a theme park
Great America one might say
We shared hours of joy and happiness day after day
Until one day all the joy stopped
And the happiness came to an end
My lover no longer wanted to be lovers anymore
She only wanted to be friends

Finding the Spirit

Thank You oh heavenly Father for receiving me into Thine
Kingdom and for the tuff love that has humbled me, but has not
Allowed me to fall off into the hands of satan, I pray Thine Holy
Spirit remains in me for it is to easy for my flesh too follow the
Way of the wicked and without Thine discipline I would surely
Be fooled into believing what is false, bless me to understand the
Truth so that I may change the wrong ways in which I sin into
Ways in which I win the heart of my glorious God

Sucker For Love

I'm a sucker for love a sucker for love
How much of a sucker can I be
Maybe twice the fool as the average man
For I was already blessed to see love
But I didn't recognize the game then
So I didn't know it would be love
I didn't know I would need love
I surely didn't know I was a sucker

Seeking Vision

Thank You oh God for the messengers You have sent to me
Though I have eyes I can not decode what I see and though
I have ears I can not comprehend what I hear but
It is because of Your blessings that I am able to move
Forward without fear, dear God I pray I will be able
To look past a persons fronts and read the true purpose
In which they present themselves in my presence
To prevent satans posse from stopping Thy plan
Be my eyes and ears Lord so I will have enough sense
To trust in Thee

Revelations of Self

Life is a dream
If you live for me
I'd give the whole world
And show my love be true to you
What would I do
If you'd eat, sleep and breathe for me
I'd change your whole world
And show our love to be true
Imagine that me and you
Can you imagine that me and you

Seeking Completion

Thank You Lord for a new life, I pray to You oh God
For strength, for I am weak, confused and can not
Comprehend certain situations, bless me Lord
With infinite wisdom so that I may gain understanding
And acknowledge the truth of Self to the world
Thank You Lord for taking control of my life
And freeing me from the worries I face
For I would rather deny myself and follow You my Lord
Than to possess everything and live in fear knowing
One day it will all be gone, thank You Father for a new day

Too Be One Hundred Percent Committed

If one hundred percent commitment is what it takes
Miss lady can you tell me what I'm suppose to do
For us too stand in this aisle and join our fate when
You got a man I understand but still want to get close
To you, oh I'm nervous now but I can't wait, I'm not
Trying to break up a happy home so I pop champagne
Too lift up that veil and see your face, I pour out a
Toast for you and your man, but its not just your
Pretty face that I love and it is a lucky man who
Has the chance to make you his wife, you can start
From your feet and go through all the above, so I wish
You well the finest things the best in life, you're so much
Like a blessing that floated down from the skies and in
My payers I pray for you that he treats you right, once
Again I thank You Lord for hearing my cries, I pray
His love is true, but I'm on the outside looking in for a
Woman too whom I'm so perfectly fitted so can you
Please tell me what I'm suppose to do too be blessed

Finding Assistance

Thank You Lord for sharing with me the feelings
That are in Your heart, I pray to Thee oh God that
I will be able to withstand the anguish caused by
Sinners whom fail to repent and react to them with
The same compassion that has been shown too me
Through my Lord and Savior, bless me oh God to
Not become confused by the things that my finite
Mind can not comprehend and strengthen my faith
So that I can have total trust in Thee even if I can
Not comprehend every circumstance I can have
Comfort in knowing the outcome has been caused
By God and is acceptable to be right

Lifes Biggest Decision

I would rather have death than
All the money in the world
If I were to have no companion
For money owns no feelings
It would rather be spent than
Anything else that's all its good for
A few good times but
What happens when its gone
Its going to take a real good love song
To get it back if you're lucky but
I don't trust my luck to no blackjack

Finding I AM

Thank You Lord for allowing me to acknowledge Self
I pray for Your continuous support oh God for without
The support of Your hand my feet would not move to
The path of the righteous and my legs would not be able
Too withstand the persecution and oppression of man
Bless me dear God to be one in the body of Christ so that
I may live to complete Thy purpose and not just for selfish
Reasons, grant me the consciousness to remember
Your ways Lord so that I never again become lost in Self
And never loose the light too lead others out of darkness

Sucker For My Lost Love

I'm a sucker for love a sucker for love
My love and I were like a theme park
How much of a sucker can I be
Great America on might say
Maybe twice the fool as the average man
We shared hours of joy and happiness day
After day, for I was already blessed to see
Love, until one day all the joy stopped
But I didn't recognize the game then
And the happiness came to an end
I didn't know it would be love
My lover no longer wanted to be lovers anymore
I didn't know I would need love
She only wanted to be friends
I surely didn't know I was a sucker

I AM Finding Vision

Thank You oh God for the Holy Spirit, Lord I pray
You use me to enlighten the lives of others so they too
Can sing praises in Thy holy name, bless me with
Your presence dear God, for these roads I walk are ruff
And full of snares but not once will I worry or become
Scared, You are my Savior so I will always be prepared
Through prayer I know all my needs are taken care
Although I can't help but live in sin in such a sinful world
Staying out of stuff that don't smell so good
Seems impossible until I see the sun shining clearly
In my path allowing me to step over to a clean place

Please Spare Me No Pain

In these words I offer my heart, my love and my
Self, to you to do as you please spare me no pain
I'm used to the game
Years gone by and things still the same
I feel a revolution coming
I want you to be a part of that change
So in these words I place my heart, my love and my
Self with feelings to strong to be held by these lines
For they are more than just lines to me
From my heart I bring the passion
A gift of love, to you to start a new day with Myself
With the love that comes from my heart, I offer
Myself to you to start a new day, and today
This day I prepare Myself to start a new day
With my heart my love
And in these words I offer my heart, my love and my
Self to you to do as you please spare me no pain
Please spare me no pain

Seeking Paradise

Thank You Lord for Your love, I pray to You oh God
For discipline so that when the wind blows my ways
Will not waver but remain constant as I make my way
Closer to You my God, Lord I pray that You do not
Allow my pride to prevent me from perceiving the truth
Of Thy laws and that You look past my perfectionist ways
Placing Your penetrating gaze upon my heart
All praises I sing for Thee provider of my peace
Producer of my prosperity and presenter of my gift

Questions

What would you do if you woke up
And your heart was gone?
Would you think I stole it? What if I did?
Would you ask for it back?
Or would you think someone else took it?
What would you give to live life with me?
What's on your mind?
Would you like to share it with me?
When can I see you again?
Do I have to steal your heart?
Why do you think they call me Konvik?
What do you believe in?
How do you feel about love?
How deep do you think I can get?
Why do you think they call me Stallion?
Do you want to know me?
What do you want from me?
What about us wrapped up in a line?
How do you think that sounded?
Do you think I'm crazy?
What do you dream about?
Did I ask when can I see you again?
Can you help me make sense of all this madness?
What do you think about me?
Would you like one more question?
What do you want to ask me?
Will you answer all these questions?
Are you ready for a new beginning?
Do you know how to cook?
What is it you don't like?
Will I be on your mind all night?
What time is it?
Will you ever get tired of me?
Do you want any more questions?
Will you be afraid to ask or
Will you be afraid to answer???

Seeking Answers

Thank You Lord for the freedom to choose
Bless me oh God to choose the right path
So that I do not trespass against another and
That I may forgive those who trespass against me
Lord I pray for forgiveness for this world of sin that
I was born into, thank You sweet Jesus for saving me
From my sins, bless me Lord with sacrifice so that
I maybe as Christ in my ways, mind, body and spirit
With all my heart I sing praises to Thee

Genesis of Self
Life is a dream
I live for you
I'd give the whole world
If your love be true
What would I do
I'd eat, sleep and breathe for you
I'd change your whole world
If the love be true
Imagine that me and you
Dreaming about change

Finding Completion
Thank You Lord for supplying for my needs
I pray You use me oh God as a tool to fix this world
Into the mold that has been designed ages ago
Lord, bless me with discipline so that I remain obedient
To Thy love and never folding in to temptation
Too destroy my home, bless me Lord with understanding
Of the wisdom that You have bestowed upon me
I pray for certainty in the decisions I make that affect
My life and also the lives of others

Return
Too
A
New
Beginning

A Testimony Too Self

How can I turn back now that I have begotten thy book. I will not turn back if it is clear. To insure clarity I shall prepare a fast. Then we shall see thy kingdom coming. During the fast I shall seek out the knowledge of thine vision. This is thy testimony to thine Self, hold it within thine soul and speak it only as the truth, in order not too deceive your brother who is indeed thine Self. For all that is in the Heavens and on the Earth is by the love of God, so it is wise to give thanks and praise to God. Who is the merchant of mercy, but God that gives freely to whom He will. I pray You give unto me oh God, for I give all praise to Thee for Thine glory. Thanks be to God for the breath I breathe as a means of life. Without You oh God I would have been stillborn waiting too die again, but with You oh God I have been given a chance too live. I pray that I live not by chance, but by Your will which Thee merciful has placed in me at birth. I shall not cease to work until I receive my lot in thy land and my place in Thine kingdom.

Future books by Andre Pullen:

"Poetry in Parables
A Testament of My Crazy Life"
A book of poetry containing the poems in "SVPnP Return too a New Beginning," also including additional work that offers more insight to the mind of the author. Minus the prayers/meditations included in "SVPnP" this book is of equal without the religious intensity.
Coming Soon

"Self Visions of Psalms of Praise
Songs From the Book of Self"
A book containing over five times as many affirmations included in "SVPnP Return too a New Beginning." This book will be of huge assistance for the person seeking to live a more spiritual life. If you are inspired or touched by the prayers/meditations in "SVPnP" this book will be a great delight and a must have for you.
Coming Soon 2003

How to contact the author
Self Vision, (Andre Pullen) is available for readings and speeches for businesses, associations and various organizations. Request and any inquiries should be directed to the address below. Comments, questions and opinions from readers are also welcomed and encouraged by the author.

Andre Pullen
A Vision Publishing
P.O. Box 900
Chicago Heights, Il 60412-0900

Share a blessing with a friend or family member by sending them a copy of *"Self Visions of Poetry in Parables, Return Too a New Beginning."* To order send check or money order for $13.95 plus shipping to the address listed below.

Name:

Address:

City: State: Zip:

Number of books: x $13.95   = $
        Shipping: x $2.00 per book   = $
                                  Total   = $

Please make check or money order payable to:

    A Vision Publishing
    P.O. Box 900
    Chicago Heights, Il 60412-0900

Please allow 4 to 6 weeks for delivery

Order your favorite poem or prayer for yourself or a friend on ¼ page laminated cards and stickers or on 2x8in. laminated bookmarkers. (Some longer poems may not be fitting for bookmarkers) List poems and prayers on back or separately. Custom framing also available, send form for inquiries with contact info.

Laminated $1.50 and 4/$5
Stickers $2.00 and 4/$7
Add 75 cents for shipping on orders less than $14 and $1.50 on orders more than $14

Total # of poems   Total $

Name:

Address:

City: State: Zip:

Comments

Please make check or money order payable to:
        A Vision Publishing
        P.O. Box 900
        Chicago Heights Il 60412

Please allow 4 to 6 weeks for delivery